NATIONAL GEOGRAPHIC

Our Town

Faridah Yusof

Our town used to be very small.

Now it is much bigger.
Many people moved to the town.
The town has grown and changed.

There used to be lots of open space around our town.

Now there are lots of houses.
People built more houses as the town grew.

There used to be dirt roads in our town.

Now there are paved roads.
People built the paved roads as the town grew.

There used to be only a few stores in our town.

Now there are many stores.
People built more stores as the town grew.

There used to be one small school in our town.

Now there are many large schools.
People built more schools as the town grew.

Do you know how your town used to look?